COLLECTING
POT-LIDS

ISBN 0 905447 06 9 (Paperback only)
ISBN 0 905447 05 0 (Hardback only) 241

Text set in 11 pt. Photon Times and Univers, printed
by photolithography, and bound in Great Britain at
The Pitman Press, Bath

BALL, A.   ~~738·38~~ 738·17 HANLEY   15.9.77.

Collecting pot-lids.   £2.50.   IN STORE

RETURN OR RENEW BY LAST DATE SHOWN

OCT 1977   28. APR 00

03 DEC 84

12. NOV
12 JUL 1996

10. NOV 99

1/12/99 Su

FOR RENEWALS QUOTE DETAILS ABOVE AND DATE
DUE FOR RETURN. A CHARGE IS MADE FOR OVERDUE
BOOKS.

STAFFORDSHIRE COUNTY LIBRARY

0 905447 05 0

2/1/003/75

0905 447 050 241 CF

*Coloured pot-lid:
"Exhibition Buildings of
1851", 2 star (actual
size). Overleaf: part of
enlarged detail of lid
taken from original
copper plate engraving.*

COLLECTING POT-LIDS

Coloured, Black & White with
Current Price Trends

by

A. Ball

738·17

MAB PUBLISHING
458c, Stanton Road, Burton-upon-Trent
Staffs. DE15 9RS. England

The Author

As a child A. Ball lived only a few hundred yards from the premises of one of the largest manufacturers of pot-lids. He did not appreciate this until years later, by which time he had left Stoke-on-Trent. He subsequently discovered his great grandfather had worked at the actual Pratt factory.

Mr. Ball and his wife have since built-up a unique collection of pot-lids over the past thirty years – a collection which is probably the best in the world. They have an interest in all antiques of the Victorian period and also have fine collections of Baxter prints, fairings and paperweights.

Mr. Ball is the author of *The Price Guide to Pot-lids*, *The Price Guide to Baxter Prints* (with M. Martin), and *So You Think You Know Your Antiques* (with Leslie Crowther). He has written numerous articles for antique magazines all over the world. He is Secretary of the "Pot-Lid Circle".

Contents

Cover Photograph

Top, left to right: "Patey and Co., Bears Grease": G;
"Wellington": 5 star; "Blanch Flower—Great Yarmouth:
F; Bottom, left to right: "The Donkey's Foal: 2 star;
"Queen's Head": F; "Thompson, Walters, Hole and Co.;
Cherry Toothpaste": F.

6

Introduction

The purpose of this book is to introduce "pot-lids" to not only new collectors but also to, hopefully, increase the knowledge of existing collectors, by explaining the background and history of the origin of those colourful small items of ceramic ware so popularly known by the term 'pot-lids'.

Since civilisation began, the human race has always been attracted by colour, and the wish to have possessions which were colourfully decorated has never changed. However, to produce colour can often be very expensive, both in terms of time and money, so that when transfer-printing was discovered to be a practical proposition in the mid-eighteenth century, the innovation was warmly received by everyone.

"Pompey and Caesar",
4 star.

This illustration is a print taken from the original copper plate engraving used in the manufacture process as are the other black-and-white il-lustrations of lids in this book.

This picture was taken from Sir Edwin Landseer's painting "The Cavalier's Pets". The plume in the hat can be white, red and white, or blue and red.

7

Methods of Manufacture

The method of production made possible the introduction of reproducing a picture or lettering on ceramic wares on a repetitive basis, and at considerably reduced cost on the previous method of decorating by hand on an individual basis. This new and cheaper system of decorating was achieved by engraving a copper plate with the subject to be shown, then inking in the engraved plate with the colour required, usually either blue, sepia, black, violet, or green, from which a tranfer would then be taken. This transfer would then be applied to the surface of the article being decorated, after which it would be glazed and then fired in the kiln to fix the colour. This can very easily be verified by reference to the blue and white wares seen today and referred to as "Willow Pattern".

As mentioned previously, this method of decoration proved successful and very popular, but there was still one very important drawback, all articles so decorated were only seen in one colour, i.e. monochrome. How much of an improvement it would be if these articles being decorated could be shown in more than one colour, i.e. polychrome.

In following the development of colour-printing, the name of George Baxter comes to the fore. In the early part of the nineteenth century, he took out a patent to do just this, by basing his idea on the previous method, but by including more blocks/copper plates, each block or plate carrying a separate colour, then completing the picture by super-imposing each plate or block over each other. To describe this process in its entirety would take enough space for a book in itself, so only the bare facts are given, to serve as an introduction to how colour – printing came to be introduced on the ceramic items known as "Pot Lids".

Experiments, based on George Baxter's patent, had been taking place in the Potteries, with the glittering prospect of affluence to the person who could achieve this aim of producing wares printed in more than one colour, and it is known that one of Geo. Baxter's workmen, Alfred

8

Reynolds, left him after serving an apprenticeship, and took up a position in the Potteries about 1846. This date is significant because this is just about the period when the first colour-printed wares were produced, and it seems rather more than coincidence that these two methods were so similar in application. Given this background, the knowledge of Alfred Reynolds, the facilities and the skills of the artists and engravers as employed in the Potteries, it only remained to the discretion of several far-seeing persons, as to how to develop this marvellous innovation of producing colour-printed wares at a price to be afforded by the masses.

Three factories are known to have been very successful in producing under-glass colour-printed wares, these were F. & R. Pratt & Co., J. Ridgway & Co., and T. J. Mayer, all situated in the Potteries.

In charge of the engravers at Messrs. F. &. R. Pratt, was a very capable and talented engraver/artist named Jesse Austin, b. 1806–d. 1879, who saw the possibilities of using this process of colour printing in extending the interests of F. &. R. Pratt by using the method to increase the sales of items produced by Pratt's who, at that particular period, were engaged in supplying large quantities of pots to the medicinal trade and other allied products.

In describing the contents of these pots, two methods were used, one which had a paper label over the lid and pot, whilst the other would be printed, giving, most probably, both the name of the manufacturer and the contents; incidentally, this second method never really went out of fashion, possibly because of the economic price, and was used contemporary with the multi-coloured printed lids, production actually continuing up to the 1930's.

Jesse Austin saw this as an excellent opportunity to increase sales, by making these pots more acceptable to their customers. This he achieved by basically making use of Geo. Baxter's process and adapting this system for use on ceramic wares. However, there was a very difficult

"Our Pets", 4-star; on the
left the diamond shows
the date of registration as
29th March 1852.

problem for him to overcome before any colour-printed wares could be produced, namely, Geo. Baxter held a patent which only permitted his method to be used by licence holders.

We have previously mentioned that Geo. Baxter dissected his picture into the colours required, he then superimposed these sectional prints over the outline picture, thereby building up to a completed colour-print. Jesse Austin overcame this problem by following this process, with one main difference, he applied the outline print last, which meant that he also dissected his picture in to the colour required, but with greater efficiency, he only used red, yellow and blue, with occasionally green or damson, and using black/brown for his outline plate. He then applied this outline plate over the previously applied sectionalised colour-plates, which, in effect, reversed Geo. Baxter's patent.

The original and actual process was extremely arduous for the production teams concerned, and was only in operation for approximately fifty years, after which still cheaper methods were introduced, but we are rather fortunate today in being able to see lids being produced, using the original tools and the system employed. This is possible, owing to a contemporary well-known manufacturer deciding to re-issue certain well known prints on lids to be issued for collectors, and a visit to the manufacturer concerned, enabled the following details to be noted.

Three people were actively engaged on this work, one printer and two transferrers. The printer mixes his own colours from an old recipe book, this is done by mixing oil with dry colour powder until it is the required consistency. He then spreads the colour completely over the plate to be used, filling in all the engraved sections, after which he scapes away all the colour, leaving the engraved sections filled. This copper-plate usually has two engravings of the subject being produced, obviously it is cheaper to produce two at any one time.

The colour used for the first transfer in this instance

"The Enthusiast", 2-star; this illustration was taken from a painting by Theodore Lane.

being buff. The plate, being prepared, a sheet of special tissue paper is placed over the engraved plate and both are then passed through a hand-press very similar to an old-

THE ENTHUSIAST

fashioned mangle. This operation made one realise how quickly a plate can wear after such treatment as this.

This tissue is now passed to a transferrer, and, of course, it is realised that this section of the print is now on the tissue in question. This girl cuts out the section required, approximately the size of the lid, and carefully places this over the surface of the lid to be used, which is still in its "biscuit" state, that is, before being glazed and fired. She then presses and dabs with a special hand-type of round brush, finishing off with a cloth and a wet sponge, which effectively removes all traces of paper, leaving the impression on the lid. Perhaps it should be mentioned here, that at no time during these operations is any colour seen, everything looks a drab brown. After this first process, exactly the same operation is followed for colour No. 2, in this case it was blue, followed again by pink No. 3, and finally by the outline No. 4.

The next stage was to transfer the back-stamp on each lid after which comes the process of "hardening", which entails firing the lids for approximately 10 hours at a temperature of 750°. This removes all the oil from the colours. After removal from the kiln and when cooled down, each lid is then dipped in glaze and again fired for a period of 12 hours at a temperature of 1120°. This is the stage at which the colours are brought out in all their brilliance and all this work seems justified, but unfortunately this is not the completion, each lid has gold incorporated in the back-stamp plus certain decorative gold items, and this means a further firing at a lower temperature of 750°. If the gold was added during earlier firings, it would not stand up to the necessary heat, resulting in running and melting.

It must also be realised that this stage of producing pot-lids is only a part of the whole, starting with a drawing, through to engraving copper-plates. Incidentally, the printer concerned, said that he thought it would take about 4–6 months to engrave a set of the plates as used by him for this job.

HIGH LIFE

BE SURE THE HAND MOST DARING THERE, HAN WIPED AWAY A TEAR.

EMBARKING FOR THE EAST

"High Life", 1-star; taken from a painting by Sir Edwin Landseer. "Embarking for the East", 3 star; without chain border, 2 star.

Manufacturers

Having now established the production methods, the next and very important question is, "Who produced what?"

We know that the production was confined mainly to F. &. R. Pratt &. Co., of Fenton, Stoke-on-Trent, with competitors in T. J. &. J. Mayer of Longport, Stoke-on-Trent, and J. Ridgway & Co., of Shelton, Stoke-on-Trent. These three firms account for the major output of pot-lids and ware, and a brief history of these three firms can now be outlined, showing the development of colour-printed ware, until it ceased.

J. Ridgway & C., 1830–55.

J. Ridgway, Bates & Co., 1855–58 (pot-lids produced).

Bates, Brown-Westhead, Moore & Co., 1858–61 (pot lids produced and J. Austin employed for short period).

Brown, Westhead, Moore & Co., 1862–1904 (pot-lids discontinued but occasional re-issues).

Name changed to Cauldon Ltd., in 1905 and, in 1920, took over its major competitor F. &. R. Pratt, with all its assets, including the original copper plates used for transfer-printing. Trading continued until 1960, when Cauldon, in turn, was taken over by Coalport, who are now part of the Wedgwood group.

T. J. &. J. Mayer were in business from 1842–55, during which period they commenced making pot-lids and ware. Their fortunes varied over the years, and a number of different owners were implicated until, in 1890, all the assets were acquired by Kirkhams of Stoke-on-Trent, who used the original copper-plates to re-issue collectors items of pot-lids. This was the situation until Portmeirion took over the factory in 1962, and all re-issues were discontinued.

So now, a comparatively full picture can be outlined by stages:

1. Originals are lids or ware which were produced for their named purpose.

2. These items are referred to as "early" or "late", according to the period as mentioned previously.
3. Approx. dates:

> Very early, 1845–1860
> Early, 1860–1875
> Late, 1875–1900

4. Re-issues (which were never used as lids) 1900-up to the present time.
5. Details to help in deciding which category to place a lid:

   (a) *Very early.* Flat top, small crazing, usually either Bear or Pegwell Bay subjects and generally good colours.

   (b) *Early.* Convex top, small to large crazing, generally good colours.

   (c) *Late.* Heavier in texture, usually poorer colours, larger and more uniform crazing.

   (d) *Re-issues from Kirkhams.* Flat tops, no crazing, two holes in top rim for hanging purposes, very heavy in texture, and could have an inscription on the underside stating "Coloured prints from the original plates engraved for the Jesse Austin process 1845–1870. Reproduced by Kirkhams Ltd., Stoke-on-Trent, England. 1947". Collectors should beware of any lids which have either been painted over or filled in with plaster on the underside.

   (e) *Re-issues from Cauldon.* A lighter texture becoming more like porcelain, usually of a creamy nature. Could have large crazing and details on the reverse stating "This picture is printed from the original engravings used for the Old English Pot Lids made by F. &. R. Pratt of Fenton about 1850–1860".

   (f) *Re-issues from Coalport.* At the present time, Coalport are issuing modern re-issues in limited editions. These are clearly marked as such and are printed on a china (porcelain) body, as distinct from the older pottery used originally. The lids are The Waterfall, St. Pauls and River Pageant, Bear Hunting, The Dentist, The Maid-Servant, The Swing, Village Wakes, Parish Beadle, and Xmas Eve.

These remarks should enable the amateur collector to be a little more discriminating when choosing a lid for his/her collection, and maybe help when deciding on a suitable price to pay.

Black-and-white lid: group C.

ANCHOVY PASTE
For SANDWICHES &c.
BY APPOINTMENT
PURVEYORS to Her MAJESTY
PREPARED BY
CROSSE & BLACKWELL
ESTABLISHED 21 SOHO SQUARE IN 1706
LONDON

Uses of Pot-Lids

Having now established "who produced lids" and "how lids were produced", it remains to confirm who used these colourful pictoral lids, and for what purpose.

The first recorded items of ware which were used for this new method of decoration were the now so well-known pots which contained "Bears Grease", this was a prepartion as used on the hair, for both preservation and grooming.

The recorded variations of multi-coloured lids with a bear motif is approximately twenty-four, with at least as many of the monochrome lids, but whereas the multi-colour ones were only produced from about 1846, for approximately fifty years, the monochrome ones were in production contemporary with, and possibly up to, 1930.

The use to which these pots could be put presented an infinite variety, and very shortly after the introduction of under-glaze multi-colour printing, it was realised that this colourful advertising method could be used very profitably on lids used for pots containing meat or fish pastes, and two small manufacturers of shrimp and fish pastes, based at Pegwell Bay, a small fishing village on the east coast of England near to Margate, promptly took advantage of the situation and, records show that the two firms mentioned, S. Banger and Tatnell & Son, ordered vast quantities of pots and lids which were designed and produced solely for the specialised market of their own fish products. There are at least sixty varieties of these Pegwell Bay lids, all of which show scenes connected with the fishing industry in this area, and also the allied trade of manufacturing fish pastes.

Other manufacturers of these allied products, such as meat paste manufacturers Crosse & Blackwell, quickly followed suit and by the 1850's there was a very thriving industry in these pots with such colourful lids.

Cosmetic manufacturers also saw the possibilities in the use of this new idea of printed decorative pots, and various kinds of "cold cream", "powders" and "salves" were presented in pots with very colourful lids of floral design.

In addition to all the lids designed to show the contents of the pots, manufacturers were alert to exploit the situation whereby contemporary news or details of prominent personages could be used to the best advantage.

Black-and-white pot-lids showing various uses:
1 C; 2 A; 3 D; 4 B; 5 D;
6 C; 7 C; 8 C; 9 D.

19

Sources of Illustrations

1851 saw the opening of the Great Exhibition in Hyde Park, London, and this was an opportunity not to be missed. A series of exhibition subject lids were produced and obviously this proved a success because over the next few years lids were produced showing scenes, not only from the 1851 Exhibition, but from the New York Exhibition of 1853, the International Exhibition of 1862, Paris Exhibitions of 1867 and 1878, and the Philadelphia Exhibition of 1876.

A series of six lids were produced showing scenes with Shakespearian interests, such as Anne Hathaway's Cottage, Shakespeare's House (interior), Shakespeare's House (exterior), Holy Trinity Church (Stratford-upon-Avon), Hamlet and His Fathers Ghost and Seven Ages of Man.

Numerous lids were sold which showed portraits of popular or famous people in the news, just to mention a few: there are several different varieties showing Queen Victoria, Queen Victoria and Prince Albert, and Prince Albert as a memorial lid on the occasion of his death in 1861; the Duke of Wellington seemed to be one of Her Majesty's favourite subjects, there are at least ten different pictures of the Duke seen on lids. Obviously the original copper-plates became very worn due to continual use and, when reconditioning became necessary, some detail would either be omitted or added.

Other personalities whose likeness is committed to posterity on lids are:

Harriett Beecher Stowe, the American authoress of *Uncle Tom's Cabin*, who visited England, in approximately 1853, for support for her anti-slavery campaign.

Garibaldi, the Italian freedom fighter who visited England in 1864.

Napolean III and Empress Eugenie were married in 1853, and this was another occasion to be recorded on a lid.

The Prince of Wales visited the tomb of George Washington in 1860, this again was an event to be recorded.

In 1863, the Prince of Wales married Princess Alexandra of Denmark, this event is shown, not only on a lid, but also on a meat paste jar which shows the procession at the reception.

The Allied Generals concerned in the Crimea War were the subjects for several lids; also Sir Robert Peel, the politician who introduced the police force as we know it today (hence the nicknames "Bobbies" or "Peelers").

Public buildings came in for their share of attention, and lids are seen with pictures of Buckingham Palace, New Houses of Parliament (opened 1852), Sandringham (purchased for the Crown in 1862), Thames Embankment (built 1864–1870), Blackfriars Bridge (built 1865–1869), Holborn Viaduct (built 1867–1869), New St. Thomas's Hospital (built 1870–1871).

These, and other buildings seen on lids, were used as a means of not only disseminating information, but obviously another means of selling more pots of whatever product was being sold.

Apart from the named lids mentioned there were many others which were used and it is perfectly clear that the more popular the subject, the more pots would be sold; there are numerous examples of this, by reference to lids or ware which show copies of adaptions from popular paintings of the period.

Detail of part of the "Allied Generals" (actual size), 3 star; heightened in gold, 4 star; with gold marbled pot complete, 6 star.

"Trafalgar Square",
2 *star*.

Title of Lid	Title of Painting	Painted by
Shooting Bears	Bear Hunt in the Pyrenees	
The Shrimpers	The Prawn Fishers	
	The Young Shrimpers	W. Collins, R. A.
Tyrolese Village Scene	St. Goar on the Rhine	
The Stone Jetty	The Homeward Bound	F. R. Lee, R.A.
The Toilette	Interior of Dutch House – later half of 17th Century	Casper Netscher
Bay of Naples	Bay of Naples – Early Morning	W. Callow
Great Exhibition, 1851	Great Exhibition Polka – 1851	
Great Exhibition, 1851		
Closing Ceremony		W. Simpson
Queen Victoria on Balcony	Baptism of the Prince of Wales, in St. George's Chapel, Windsor	Sir George Hayter
G. Victoria & Albert Edward		R. Thorburn
Late Duke of Wellington		Count D'Orsay
Funeral of the late Duke of Wellington	Funeral of the late Duke of Wellington	G. Baxter
The Blue Boy	The Blue Boy	T. Gainsborough, R.A.
Dr. Johnson	Dr. Johnson in the ante-room of Lord Chesterfield	E. M. Ward, A.R.A.
Windsor Park or returning from Stag-Hunting	Windsor Park or returning from Stag-Hunting	G. Baxter
Trafalgar Square	The Nelson Column	G. Hawkins
Thirsty Soldier		
The Irishman	The Tired Soldier	F. Goodall
War	War	Wouvermann
Peace	Peace	Wouvermann
Conway Castle	Conway Castle	H. Gastineau
War	War	Sir E. Landseer
Peace	Peace	Sir E. Landseer
May Day Dancers at the Swann Inn	May Day	
Pet Rabbits	The Pet Rabbits	
Il Penseroso	Il Penseroso	T. Webster, R. A.
Parish Beadle	The Parish Beadle	D. Wilkie, R. A

"The Best Card", 2 star;
with decorative border,
3 star; taken from the
painting of the same title
by Burnett.

THE BEST CARD

Title of Lid	Title of Painting	Painted by
The Village Wedding	The Village Wedding	D. Teniers
The Buffalo Hunt	An Indian Buffalo Hunt	G. Catlin
The Enthusiast	The Enthusiast	T. Lane
Chief's Return from Deer-stalking		Sir E. Landseer
The Best Card	The Best Card	J. Burnett
Hide and Seek	Hide and Seek	R. T. Ross, R.S.A
A Fix	Playing Draughts	J. Burnett
The Game Bag	The Cover Side	F. R. Lee, R.A.
Children Sailing Boat in Tub	Contrary Winds	T. Webster, R. A.
Good Dog	The Friends	Sir E. Landseer, R.A.
The Begging Dog	The Beggar	Sir E. Landseer, R.A.
Pompey and Caesar	The Cavaliers Pets	Sir E. Landseer, R.A.
High Life	High Life	Sir E. Landseer, R.A.
Low Life	Low Life	Sir E. Landseer, R.A.
The Snow-Drift	Highland Shepherd's Dog in Snow	Sir E. Landseer, R.A.
The Skewbald Horse		P. Wouvermann
The Cottage Children	Cottage Children	T. Gainsborough
Lady, Boy and Goats	Harvest Time in the Scottish Highlands	Sir E. Landseer and Sir A.W. Callcott
Lend a Bite	Lending a Bite	W. Mulready, R.A.
The Dentist	The Dentist	Isach Van Ostade
The Farriers	The Smithy	P. Wouvermann
The Times	The Newspaper	T. S. Cord
Uncle Toby	Uncle Toby and The Widow	C. R. Leslie, R.A.
The First Appeal	The First Appeal	F. Stone
The Second Appeal	The Second Appeal	F. Stone
The Trooper	The Trooper	Herring, Baxter and Bright
Street Scene on the Continent	Utrecht	G. Jones, R.A.
Peasant Boys		Murille
Strawberry Girl		Reynolds
The Last In		W. Mulready, R.A.
The Truant		T. Webster
The Hop Queen		W. T. Withrington, R.A.

Factors Affecting Prices

In addition to the details mentioned, there are several other very important factors to be recognised when deciding whether to add to ones collection, these are:

1. Lids should be printed in good colourings, pale lids are not so acceptable.
2. Registration should be perfect.
3. Damaged lids should allow for any damage in the price.
4. Restoration should be taken into account.
5. If possible, always check with the points mentioned previously in arriving at a decision regarding early or late – the earlier lids are usually better.
6. Most important of all is the question of rarity.

It is obvious that with such a large quantity of lids being produced, certain ones would be more popular than others, and this is why there is a wide difference in price.

The range could vary from where many hundreds of a particular lid can still be found, to where there is only one off recorded. Among the rarest are flower lids and such as Washington, Buffalo Hunt, Matador, Bears Grease Manufacturer, How I Love To Laugh, Eastern Lady and Black Attendant, and many others.

Lids which can be seen in most collections are: Village Wedding, Uncle Toby, Garibaldi, Strasbourg, On Guard, Dr. Johnson, Shakespeare's House, War, Peace and many others too numerous to mention.

Price Guide
Coloured Pot-Lids

To help one to decide on rarity category, the following list of coloured lids will be of assistance.

All commoner lids will be marked with one star, and others marked with two or more stars, with six stars being the rarest.

Where numbers are given, they relate to the numbers as given in *The Price Guide to Pot Lids* (A. Ball).

Basic guides to judging values on a rarity basis are:

	£
One star	15– 30
Two stars	25–50
Three stars	40–100
Four stars	75–150
Five stars	100–200
Six stars	Price to be agreed

Left to right: "The Game Bag", 1 star; "The First Appeal", 5 star; without border, 3 star, with wording round the edge "I consent she replied ...", etc., 1 star.

"Ann Hathaways Cottage", 1 star, with scroll leaf border, 2 star; "Uncle Toby", 1 star; "The Wolf and the Lamb", 1 star.

ONE STAR

Pegwell Bay (Est. 1760)
Pegwell Bay (4 shrimpers)
Belle Vue Tavern (carriage)
Belle Vue Tavern Pegwell Bay
Pegwell Bay (Shrimpers)
Landing the Fare
New Jetty and Pier, Margate
The Harbour, Marate
Royal Harbour, Ramsgate
Nelson Crescent, Ramsgate
Walmer Castle (45)
Pretty Kettle of Fish
Lobster Sauce
Shells
Hauling in the Trawl
Examining the Nets
Landing the Catch
Mending the Nets
Fish Market
The Fishbarrow
The Shrimpers
Late Prince Consort
Garibaldi
The Blue Bloy (late issue)
Dr. Johnson
Albert Memorial
Charing Cross
New Blackfriars Bridge
Thames Embankment
Chapel Royal (both varieties)
Alexandra Palace
Trafalgar Square
Transplanting Rice
The Trooper
Fording the Stream

On Guard
Hoborn Viaduct
Battle of the Nile
Meeting of Garibaldi and Victor Emmanuel
War and Peace
Chin-chew river
Harbour of Hong Kong
Ning-Po river
Wimbledon, July 1860
Rifle Contest at Wimbledon
Shakespeare's Birthplace (exterior and interior)
Ann Hathaway's Cottage
Il Penseroso
Village Wedding
The Enthusiast
A Pair
Hide and Seek
Derby Day
The Sportsman
The Game-bag
High Life and Low Life
Snow Drift
Skewbald Horse
I See You, My Boy
French Street Scene
Cattle and Ruins
Lend a Bite
The Queen, God Bless Her
Deer Drinking
The Farriers
The Shepherdess and The Shepherd Boy
The Times

29

BELLEVUE, PEGWELL BAY

1

THE VILLAGE WEDDING

2

WAR

3

ON GUARD

4

THE BATTLE OF THE NILE

5

6

ONE STAR

Uncle Toby
First Appeal and Second Appeal
Strasbourg

Wolf and the Lamb
Preparing for the Ride

"Belle Vue Tavern" with "Banger" on underside, 1 star, with small lettering and "Tatnell" on underside, 3 star.

All 1 star: 1 "Bellvue, Pegwell Bay"; 2 "The Village Wedding"; 3 "War"; 4 "On Guard"; 5 "The Battle of The Nile"; 6 "The Farriers", with gold band, 5 star.

31

*"Fair Sportswoman",
2 star; with gold edging
and maroon base com-
plete, 5 star.*

TWO STAR

Alas, poor Bruin
Bear Pit
Bears at School
Bears on Rocks
Pegwell Bay (24)
Still-life, game
Still-life, farmyard
Injury and Revenge
Fisherwomen returning home
Net-mender
River scene with boat
Foreign River scene
Swiss Riverside scene
Dutch River scene
Eastern Repast
Eastern Lady dressing hair
The Mirror
The Packman
Lady reading book
Lady with Hawk
Lady with Guitar
Lady fastening shoe
Grand. Int. Buildings, 1851
Exhibition Building, 1851
Grant Exhibition, 1851
Interior Grant Int. Building, 1851
Crystal Palace (137)
Interior View Crystal Palace
Crystal Palace (139)
Conway Castle
Seven Ages of Man
Hamlet
May Day Dancers
Children of Flora
Xmas Eve

The Swing
Blind Mans Buff
Master of the Hounds
Chiefs return from deer-stalking
Dangerous skating
Fair Sportswoman
Snap-dragon
Best Card
A Fix
The Skaters
Children Sailing Boats
Good Dog
Contrast
Feeding the chickens
Fidelity
Begging Dog
Both alike
Country quarters
Dutch winter scene
Faithful Shepherd.
Prince of Wales visiting tomb of
    Washington
Lady, Boy and Goats
Old Water Mill
International Exhibition
L'Exposition Universalle of 1867
Philadelphia Exhibition
Paris Exhibition
K. Edward and Q. Alexandra 1863
Allied Generals
Sandringham
Osbourne House
St. Pauls Cathedral and River Pageant
Strathfieldsaye
St. Pauls Cathedral (192A)

1

2

3

4

9

5

6

7

8

TWO STAR

Eleanor Cross
St. Thomas's Hospital
Golden Horn
Thirsty Soldier
Embarking for the East
Sebastopol
The Rivals
Vue de la Ville
Street scene on the Continent
The Flute Player
Vine Girl
Fisher Boy
Girl with Grapes
Tam-o-Shanter and Souter Johnny

Tam-o-Shanter
Peasant Boys
Poultry Woman
Persuasion
The Picnic
The Cavalier
The Irishmen
Red Riding Hood
Red Bull Inn
Letter from the diggings
Charity
The Listener
The Waterfall
Volunteers and Old Jack

"Vue de la Ville de Strasbourg; Prise du port", 2 star; with fancy border – 3 star.

All 2 star: 1 "Master of the Hounds"; 2 "Sandringham"; 3 "Late Prince Consort"; 4 "Interior – Crystal Palace"; 5 "Dangerous Skating"; 6 "Lady Reading Book"; 7 "Bear Pit"; 8 "Blind Man's Bluff"; 9 "The Rivals".

*"King Edward and Queen
Alexandra on their
marriage in 1863", 3 star.*

THREE STAR

Bear Hunting
Shooting Bears
The Ins
The Outs
Polar Bears
Bear, Lion and Cock
Belle Vue Tavern (29)
Pegwell Bay (32)
Pegwell Bay (Shrimping)
Still-life, fish
Sandown Castle, Kent
Walmer Castle (46)
Walmer Castle (47)
Sea Nymph with trident
The Bride
Lady, Boy and Mandoline
Lady brushing hair
Bunch of cherries
All Floral Lids
Opening Ceremony

Englands Pride
Queen Victoria and Prince Consort
Wellington (varieties)
Sir Robert Peel
Windsor Castle (178)
Windsor Park
Strathfieldsay
Napirima
Holy Trinity Church
Village Wakes
Parish Beadle
Pheasant Shooting
Breakfast Party
The Dentist
Summer and Autumn
The Maidservant
Negro and Pitcher
The Quarry
Dublin Industrial Exhibition

"The Smokers", 3 star.

P. WOUVERMANN

This fond attachment to the well known place
whence first we started into life's long race
Maintains its hold with such unfailing sway
we feel it e'en in age, and at our latest day

J. AUSTIN

OUR HOME

RIFLE CONTEST WIMBLEDON 1868

FOUR STAR

Bear attacked by dogs
Arctic Expedition
All but trapped
Belle Vue Tavern (cart)
The Toilette
Garden Terrace
The Tryst
Buckingham Palace
Windsor Castle (177)
Drayton Manor
New Houses of Parliament
Houses of Parliament (184)
Tower of London
Westminster Abbey
Trysting Place
The Lovers
Rose Garden
Ornamental Garden
Musical Trio
The Circassian
Closing Ceremony
New York Exhibition

Worlds Fair, Chicago
Queen Victoria on Balcony
Queen Victoria (Orb and Sceptre)
Edward VII and Queen Alexandra
Napoleon III and Empress Eugenie
Tria Juncta in Uno
St. Pauls Cathedral
New Houses of Parliament (entered at
stationers hall)
The Redoubt
Our Home and Our Pets
Bull Fight
Any oblong dog lid
Pompey and Caesar
Cottage Children
Mother and daughters
Royal Coat of Arms
Youth and Age
Alma
Balaclava, Inkerman and Alma
Peabody

"New Houses of Parliament", 6 star.

Opposite: 1 "French Street Scene", 1 star; 2 "Skewbald Horse", 1 star, with double gold line or seaweed band, 2 star: 3 "Our Home", 4 star; 4 "The Maidservant", 3 star; 5 "The Rifle Contest", 2 star; 6 "The Poultry Women", 2 star, with wide gold band, 6 star.

THE TIMES.

THE CHIN CHEW RIVER.

THE CAVALIER.

THAMES EMBANKMENT.

THE PARISH BEADLE. W. WILKIE

Top to bottom: "Milking the Cow", 3 star; "Tyrolese Village Scene", 3 star; "Halt near Ruins", 3 star.

Opposite: 1 "The Times", 1 star; 2 "The Chin-Chew River", 1 star; 3 "The Cavalier", 2 star; 4 "Thames Embankment", 1 star; 5 "The Parish Beadle", 3 star; 6 "Lady, Boy and Mandoline", 3 star.

1

2

FIVE STAR

Prowling Bear
Bears reading Newspaper
Bear with Valentines
Performing Bear
Pegwell Bay (23)
Dutch Fisherman
Reflection in Mirror
The Wooer
Spanish Lady
Fruit and Statue Piece
The Matador
Queen Victoria and Albert Edward

Wellington (cocked hat)
Funeral of Wellington
Sir Charles Napier
Harriet Beecher Stowe
Felix Edward Pratt
The Blue Boy
Napirima (with advertising)
A False Move
Boar Hunt
Gay Dog
Grace before meals
Strawberry Girl

"The Blue Boy", 5 star.

Opposite: 1 "Negro and Pitcher", 3 star; 2 "Cottage Children", 5 star, without malachite border, 4 star.

COLOURED POT-LIDS

1 "Strathfieldsaye, The
Seat of the Duke of
Wellington", 2 star;
2 "Holy Trinity Church,
Stratford-on-Avon",
3 star, with extra leaf and
scroll border, 5 star.

44

SIX STAR

Bears Grease Manufacturer
Attacking Bears
Bear in Ravine
Eastern Lady and Black Attendant
Jenny Lind
Meditation
Bay of Naples
Gothic Archway

Edward VII and Princess Alexandra
(128)
Royal Arms (129)
Beehive (130)
Washington crossing the Delaware
Pet Rabbits
Buffalo Hunt
How I love to laugh

"The Last In", 6 star.

Top: "The Matador",
5 star. Bottom: "Pegwell
Bay", 5 star, in one
colour only, 2 star.

"Boar Hunt", 5 star.

H.R.H. the Prince of Wales (Visiting the Tomb of Washington)

1

Chapel Royal Savoy Destroyed by Fire July 7 1864

2

I SEE YOU MY BOY

3

A PAIR.

4

5

BOTH ALIKE

6

48

"Alas Poor Bruin", 2 star;
"Xmas Eve", 2 star,
with shaped pot complete,
5 star.

Opposite: 1 "H.R.H.
Prince of Wales visiting
the Tomb of
Washington", 2 star;
2 "Chapel Royal", 2 star;
3 "I See You My Boy",
1 star; 4 "A Pair", 1 star;
5 "Garibaldi", 1 star;
6 "Both Alike", 2 star.

*"The Crystal Palace",
2 star; "Sebastopol",
2 star.*

*"Washington Crossing
the Delaware", 6 star.*

*"Examining the Nets",
1 star; "The Dentist",
3 star, with gold band
or screw top and base,
5 star.*

*"The Buffalo Hunt",
6 star.*

53

Actual size: 1 B; 2 C;
3 D.

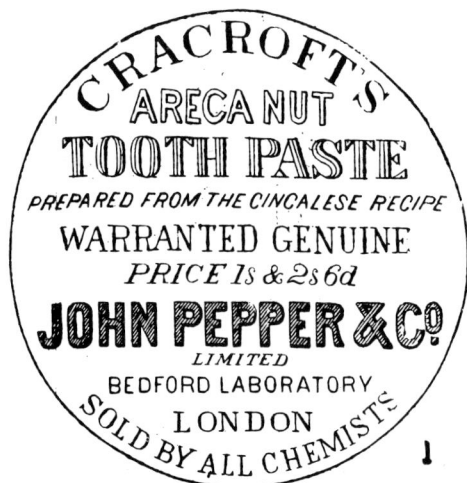

CRACROFT'S
ARECA NUT
TOOTH PASTE
PREPARED FROM THE CINCALESE RECIPE
WARRANTED GENUINE
PRICE 1s & 2s 6d
JOHN PEPPER & C?
LIMITED
BEDFORD LABORATORY
LONDON
SOLD BY ALL CHEMISTS

1

A MOORE
ROSE
COLD CREAM
Chemist
173. SLOANE ST. S.W.

2

DIPLÔME D'HONNEUR PARIS 1888
LA REINE
DES CRÈMES
BOSSARD LEMAIRE
*La seule sans rivale pour maintenir la beau
dans un perpetuel état de jeunesse et le beauté*
J LESQUENDIEU _ PARIS Frahce

3

Price Guide
Single and
2-Colour Pot-Lids

The following list will be a guide to the rarity and value of single and two-colour pot-lids. The lids have been placed into eight groups, the most common being in Group A.

Basic guides to judging values are:

	£
Group A	2– 5
Group B	5–10
Group C	10–15
Group D	15–20
Group E	20–30
Group F	30–50
Group G	50–75
Group XXX	Price by negotiation

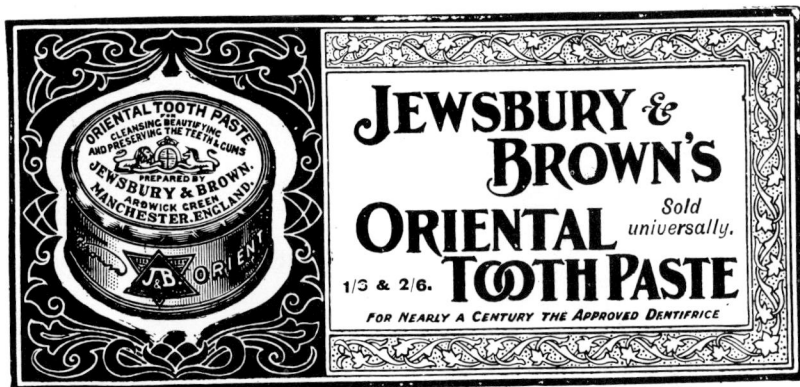

56

GROUP A

$2\frac{3}{4}''$ Caviare. Fortnum and Mason Ltd., Piccadilly, W.1.

$3\frac{1}{2}''$ Burgess's Anchovy Paste, 107 Strand.

$3\frac{1}{2}''$ Burgess's Genuine Anchovy Paste. George V coat of Arms.

$2\frac{1}{2}''$ Wood's Areca Nut, 6d size. W. Woods, Chemist, Plymouth.

$2\frac{7}{8}''$ Woods Areca Nut. W. Woods, Chemist, Plymouth.

$2\frac{5}{8}''$ Atkinson's Rose Cold Cream. 24 Old Bond St., London, 1S.

Robt. Douglas. Concentrated Egg Julop. London.

$2''$ Domed Lids. SEARCY'S Oriental Salt.

$2\frac{1}{4}''$ Flat Lid with no flange. MASON DORIN, Paris.

$2''$ Domed Lid. J. Wooley & Sons & Co. Ltd., Manchester, with trade mark of three crossed arrows set centre.

$2\frac{1}{4}''$ Domed Lid. GIRLING BROS. & Co., London.

$2\frac{7}{8}''$ Cornell & Cornell Emolline. 14 Tavern St., Ipswich.

$1\frac{3}{4}''$ Searcy Tansley & Co., Ltd. Oriental Salt.

$1\frac{3}{4}''$ Boots Cash Chemist.

1 $3\frac{1}{8}''$ B; 2 $3\frac{3}{4}''$ C; 3 $4''$ F; 4 $3\frac{1}{8}''$ B; 5 $3\frac{1}{2}''$ D; 6 $3\frac{1}{2}''$ E.

GROUP B

$3\frac{1}{2}''$ Gorgona Anchovy Paste. Army & Navy Co-op Society Ltd.
$3\frac{3}{4}''$ Keddies Real Gorgona Anchovy.
$3\frac{3}{4}''$ Keddies Bloater Paste.
$4\frac{1}{4}''$ Potted Ham with thistle trade mark.
Home Made Potted Meats. Army & Navy Co-op Society Ltd.
$3\frac{3}{4}''$ Anchovy Paste. Thistle trade mark.
$4\frac{1}{4}''$ Anchovy Paste. Thistle trade mark.
$4\frac{1}{4}''$ Bloater Paste. Thistle trade mark.
$4\frac{1}{4}''$ Potted Ham & Chicken. Thistle trade mark.
$4\frac{1}{4}''$ Thistle trade mark. No product named in panel.
Caviar. V. Benoist, Piccadilly. Large domed and fluted lid with small centre printed.
$3\frac{3}{4}''$ Saponaceous Tooth Powder. Dr. Bowditch by F. S. Cleaver.
$3''$ Oriental Toothpast. Jewsbury & Brown, Ardwick Green, Manchester.
$2\frac{3}{4}''$ Cherry. S. Maw & Son & Sons, Aldersgate St., London.
$2\frac{3}{4}''$ An Admirable Dentifrice. Cherry.
$2\frac{5}{8}''$ Cherry. Geo. Weston, Chemist, Harrogate.
$2\frac{5}{8}''$ Cherry. Boots Cash Chemist.
$3''$ Cherry. Boots Cash Chemist.
$2\frac{5}{8}''$ CRACROFT'S Areca Nut prepared from the Cingalese recipe. John Pepper & Co., Bedford Laboratory, London.
$2\frac{5}{8}''$ Commans Areca Nut. Prepared only by Commans, Bath.
$3''$ Woods Areca Nut, 1s. Size. Ornamental border.
$2\frac{5}{8}''$ "MAWS" Indian Betal Nut or Areca. S. MAW/SON & SONS.
$2\frac{5}{8}''$ BOOTS Cash Chemist. Areca Nut.
$2\frac{1}{2}''$ Pond's Areco White areca nut.
$2\frac{3}{8}''$ Calvert's Carbolic toothpaste, *sixpence.*
$2\frac{3}{8}''$ Carbolic Tooth Paste with decorative border.
$2\frac{3}{4}''$ Cherry Tooth Paste. S. Maw Son and Thompson. Aldersgate St.
$3\frac{1}{2}''$ American Dentifrice. C. R. Coffin. DDS, Baltimore.
$3''$ Boots Tooth Paste. Cash chemists.
$2\frac{1}{2}''$ Maws Indian Betel Nut or Areca Toothpaste. S. MAW SON & THOMPSON, Aldersgate St.
$2\frac{3}{4}''$ Woods Areca Nut. 6d. W. Woods, MPS.
$3''$ Areca Nut Toothpaste. An Elegant Dentifrice.
$2\frac{1}{2}''$ Areca Nut Toothpaste, – symmetrical design.

GROUP B

3″ Cherry Crown Perfumery Co. 3 banded ornamental border, trademarks crown centre.

3″ Cherry. Timothy White & Co. Chemists, Portsmouth.

3″ Cherry Tooth Paste. Timothy White Company Ltd.

$2\frac{1}{2}$″ × 3″ Lewis & Burrows Drug Stores Ltd. Areca.

Calvert's Carbolic Toothpaste. 1/9 size.

Edward Cook's Hygenic Tooth Soap. Made in England.

$2\frac{1}{4}$″ John Barker & Co. Ltd., Kensington High St. Otto of Rose.

3″ Cold Cream. The Civil Service Co-op. Soc. Ltd., 28 Haymarket.

3″ Pure Cold Cream of Roses. Army & Navy Junior Stores Ltd.

$2\frac{3}{4}$″ Cold Cream-delicately perfumed.

$2\frac{1}{2}$″ Cold Cream-delicately perfumed.

3″ Atkinson's Rose Cold Cream. 24 Old Bond Street, London, 2/6d.

3″ Atkinson's Rose Cold Cream, 24 Old Bond Street, London. 1/6d.

$2\frac{1}{4}$″ Cold Cream with ornamental background scroll.

$2\frac{1}{2}$″ Cold Cream with ornamental background scroll.

$2\frac{1}{2}$″ Cold Cream with ornamental background.

$2\frac{1}{4}$″ Cold Cream with ornamental background.

$2\frac{5}{8}$″ Cold Cream. Boots Cash Chemists.

3″ Cold Cream. Boots Cash Chemists.

$3\frac{1}{2}$″ Cold Cream of Roses. Army & Navy Co-op. Soc. Ltd.

$2\frac{3}{4}$″ Cold Cream of Roses. Army & Navy Co-op. Soc. Ltd.

$2\frac{3}{4}$″ Garrad Cold Cream of Roses. CHYMIST, Leamington.

2″ Blunt's Otto of Roses Cold Cream. J. H. Blunt & Sons, Northampton and Coventry.

$2\frac{1}{2}$″ Otto of Roses Cold Cream. Wilsons Ltd., Harrogate.

$2\frac{3}{4}$″ Allen & Hanbury. Otto of Rose Cold Cream. Plought Court, 37 Lombard St., London. E.C.4.

$2\frac{3}{4}$″ Otto of Rose Cold Cream. E. Castell Evans, MPS, Westbourne Grove (T. M. William Whiteley).

$2\frac{3}{4}$″ P. H. Maxwell. Rose Cold Cream. Chemist, Harrogate.

$2\frac{1}{2}$″ Superior Cold Cream. E. Anstee Turner, SW.

$2\frac{1}{2}$″ Cold Cream (iced effect wording).

$3\frac{1}{2}$″ Charles Rose Cold Cream. Prepared only at London, 52 Regent Street, gold rim.

$2\frac{3}{4}$″ Cold Cream. Ornamental background leaf and scroll.

$2\frac{1}{2}$″ Cold Cream. Ornamental background, scroll type.

3″ Cold Cream. Ornamental background, scallop type.

GILES COLD CREAM FOLKESTONE

1

J. CARRE CHEMIST COLD CREAM 46, BORDAGE STREET GUERNSEY

2

VIANE'S SHAVING CREAM PREPARED ONLY BY MAURICE VIANE 50, KNIGHTSBRIDGE, LONDON, S.W.1.

3

Actual size: 1 B; 2 C; 3 C.

GROUP B

$2\frac{1}{2}''$ Savory & Moores Cold Cream. 143 New Bond St., 29 Chapel St., Belgrave Square, & 1 Lancaster Gate, Hyde Park, gold rim.

$3\frac{1}{2}''$ Rose Cold Cream. Brighton & Hove Supply Assoc, Western Road, Hove, Brighton.

$3''$ Savory & Moores Cold Cream. 142 New Bond St, 29 Chapel St., Belgrave Square, 1 Lancaster Gate, Hyde Park, Ornamental border.

$2\frac{3}{4}''$ Cold Cream. Boots Cash Chemists.

$2\frac{7}{8}''$ Cold Cream of Rose. Army & Navy Co-operative.

$2\frac{7}{8}''$ Cold Cream of Rose. Army & Navy Co-operative, with black border.

$3''$ Cold Cream (iced design).

$2\frac{1}{2}''$ Cold Cream of Roses. Edward B. Stamp, 29 High St., Hampstead.

$3\frac{1}{8}''$ Timothy White Co. Otto of Rose Cold Cream. Portsmouth.

$3\frac{1}{8}''$ Timothy White Co. Otto of Rose Cold Cream. Portsmouth, with ornamental border.

$3''$ Otto of Rose Cold Cream. Timothy White Co. Ltd.

$2\frac{1}{4}''$ Cold Cream decorative scroll.

Cold Cream, wide black ornamental border.

Freke & Co., 378 Coldharbour Lane. Otto of Rose Cold Cream.

Superior Cold Cream. E. Anstee Turner, 100 & 280 Fulham Road, S.W.

Superior Rose Cold Cream. De Castro Watson & Richards, Wilton Place.

Lewis & Burrows Ltd., Rose Cold Cream. London, large border.

Godfrey & Cooke. Otto of Rose Cold Cream. 30 Conduit St., W.

Chas. E. J. Eynon. Cold Cream. 13 James St., Harrogate.

G. E. Bridge. Cold Cream. The Firs. Bournemouth.

Williams & Elvery. Cold Cream. 8 Halkin St., W., Belgrave Square.

Ellenbee Lewis & Burrows Ltd, Otto of Rose Cold Cream.

$3\frac{1}{2}''$ Almond Shaving Cream. Army & Navy Co-op. Soc. BROWN PRINT.

$4\frac{5}{8}''$ Creme De Savon In Giraud Fils Grasse. Paris, 3 gold medals.

$2''$ Troughets Corn Cure. Lighthouse trade mark, RED PRINT.

$2\frac{1}{4}''$ Dr. Wrights Pearl Ointment. Zaccheus Hunter, London.

$1\frac{3}{4}''$ Wesleys Petroleum Pomade. Blue Lid, Black Print.

$3\frac{1}{8}''$ The Patent Borax Co. Ltd., Birmingham & London.

Golden Eye Ointment. Timothy Whites & Taylors Ltd.

CH Les FAY Creme Camelia. Paris.

$2\frac{7}{8}''$ Emolline. Ipswich, Cornell & Cornell.

$2''$ Prices Ceratine. Prices Patent Candle.

Edwin Dennis. James St. & Carburton St. Stores.

J. W. Steward MPS. Medical Hall, Bridgenorth.

Searchy's Oriental Salt. Red Print.

GROUP C

$3\frac{3}{4}''$ Cream of Bloater. GILSON & SONS.
$3\frac{1}{2}''$ Burgess's Genuine Anchovy Paste. Edward VII coat of Arms. Hythe Road, Willesden.
$3\frac{3}{4}''$ Harrod's Gorgona Anchovy Paste. Harrod's Stores Ltd., 87–105 Brompton Road. BLUE PRINT.
$3\frac{1}{4}''$ Fortnum & Mason Caviar.
Fortnum & Mason Ltd., Caviar, with coat of arms. By Appt. to the King.
$3\frac{1}{4}''$ Cherry Tooth Paste. John Gosnell & Co., Extra Moist. Black & White.
$3\frac{1}{4}''$ Cherry Tooth Paste. John Gosnell & Co. *Ltd*. Extra Moist, Black and White.
$3''$ Cherry Tooth Paste. John Gosnell & Co. GREEN.
$3\frac{1}{4}''$ Cherry Tooth Paste. John Gosnell & Co. *Ltd*, GREEN.
$3''$ Jewsbury & Brown, Oriental Toothpaste. 'By Appointment'. Ardwick Green, Manchester.
$3\frac{1}{4}''$ Jewsbury & Brown. Oriental. 113 Market Street, Manchester.
$2\frac{3}{4}''$ Cherry for preserving teeth and gums. D. G. &. Co.
$2\frac{1}{2}'' \times 2\frac{1}{2}''$ Cherry Tooth Paste. Square Lid.
$3''$ Cherry Tooth Paste. Army & Navy Co-op. Society, Ltd.
$2\frac{5}{8}''$ Cherry for cleansing and preserving the teeth and gums, decorative border and background, fish, birds and fruit.
$2\frac{5}{8}''$ Wood's Cherry. RED Print. W. Woods, Plymouth.
$2\frac{1}{2}'' \times 2\frac{1}{2}''$ Areca Nut, strengthens the gums and beautifies the teeth.
$2\frac{1}{2}'' \times 2\frac{1}{2}''$ Areca nut tooth paste, strengthens the gums.
$1\frac{1}{2}'' \times 2\frac{1}{2}''$ Edward Cook's Hygenic Tooth soap, oblong lid.
$2\frac{1}{2}'' \times 2\frac{1}{2}''$ White Rose Paste. S. Maw Son & Thompson. square lid.
$2\frac{1}{2}''$ S. MAW SON & SONS. Carbolic. Aldersgate St. London.
$3''$ Areca Nut Tooth Paste.
$2\frac{3}{4}''$ Pond's American White Areca Nut Toothpaste.
$3\frac{1}{4}''$ Areco Pond's White Areca Nut Tooth Paste. C. P. Pond, Chemist, 68 Fleet St., London.
$3''$ The Areca Nut Tooth Paste. Army & Navy Co-op. Soc. Ltd.
$3''$ The Areca Nut Tooth Paste. Army & Navy Co-op. Soc. Ltd., wide grey band and gold border.
$3''$ Wood's Areca Nut. W. Woods. Plymouth. 1s. size.
$2\frac{1}{2}''$ Areca Nut. Lorimer & Co. Britannia Row. Islington, background centre design of Mosque and Lorimer trade mark.
$2\frac{3}{4}''$ Areca Toothpaste. C. S. Bowtall, Chemist, London.
$3\frac{1}{4}''$ Areca Nut Toothpaste, symmetrical design.
$3''$ Coral Toothpaste. Parker, Chemist, Uttoxeter.

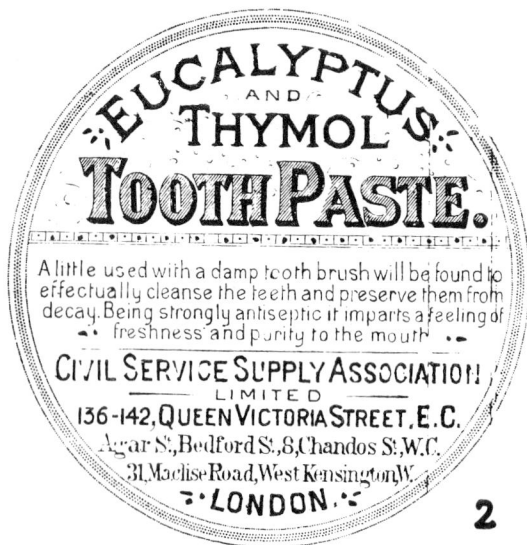

Actual size: 1 B; 2 B.

1 3″ C; 2 2½″ A;
3 3¼″ C; 4 2¾″ C;
5 2⅝″ B; 6 3½″ B;
7 2¾″ B; 8 2¾″ B.

GROUP C

4″ Coral Toothpaste. Parker, Chemist, Uttoxeter.
$2\frac{1}{2}$″ × $2\frac{1}{2}$″ square lid. White Rose Paste. S. MAW SON & SONS.
$2\frac{1}{2}$″ Cherry Tooth Paste. Lewis & Burrows Ltd. London.
3″ Cherry for Beautifying & Preserving the Teeth & Gums.
$2\frac{3}{4}$″ J. Grossmith & Son. Cherry Toothpaste, male & female head.
$2\frac{1}{2}$″ Cherry Tooth Paste. B. &. Co. Ltd., with cherry design.
$2\frac{7}{8}$″ Cherry Tooth Paste. Milburn's Ltd., Hull & Newcastle.
$2\frac{7}{8}$″ F. S. Clea. Areca Nut. 6d.
$2\frac{3}{8}$″ × $2\frac{3}{8}$″ Carbolic with ornamental border.
$2\frac{3}{8}$″ Cherry. Prepared by Geo. E. Perry, Edgbaston.
$2\frac{1}{2}$″ Cherry. Bellamy & Wakefield, Chemists, Birmingham.
$3\frac{1}{8}$″ Cherry. Harrods Stores Ltd.
$2\frac{1}{2}$″ Royal Alexandra. Cherry, Sharp Brothers, 12 & 14 Southampton Row.
3″ Zeno & Co. Cherry Tooth Paste, London.
White Carbolic. S. Maw Son & Sons, Aldersgate St.
Savars Carbolic Toothpaste.
Cherry Toothpaste for Preserving & Beautifying Teeth & Gums.
Cherry Tooth Paste for cleansing and preserving the teeth and gums, with wide
    decorative border.
Aceca Nut Tooth Paste, decorative border.
Cracrofts Areca Nut. John Pepper & Co, London, 6d.
Areca Nut Tooth Paste. Lewis & Burrows Ltd.
Cherry Toothpaste. Wm. Sutton & Co. London, ornamental border.
Tooth Paste. Ornamental Lid.
The H. C. I. Ideal Cherry Tooth Paste.
Areca Nut Toothpaste, symmetrical design centre.
Areca Nut Thooth Paste. Michael E. Foster, 50 Bishopsgate St.
Areca Nut Tooth Paste. Tomlinson Bros. Preston.
Portway & Co. Cherry Tooth Paste. 225 Jamaica Road, S.E.
Cherry Tooth Paste. Bowtall, London.
Cherry Tooth Paste, ornamental design, medium.
Cherry Tooth Paste. Co-operative, Newcastle-on-Tyne.
Oriental Tooth Paste. Co-operative. Newcastle-on-Tyne.
Antiseptic Carnation Toothpaste. W. T. Cooper, 26 Oxford St.
Pearly White for the Gums and Teeth. C. S. Bensted, Dentist.
Edward Cooks Hygenic Tooth Soap. London. E.
Savars Cherry.
George Donaldson Areca Nut. Portsea.
Fowler & Donaldson. Areca Nut. Portsea.
Pinch & Co. Areca Nut Cherry Tooth Paste, Bath.
Docteur Pierre Poudre Dentifrice, Paris.

GROUP C

Parkes Drug Stores. Cherry, London.

S. F. Goss Ltd. Cherry, London.

$2\frac{3}{4}''$ Rowlands Otto of Rose Cold Cream. Lewis & Burrows Ltd.

$2\frac{3}{4}''$ Cold Cream a la Rose. Prepared by J. B. Hay & Co. Chemists, 226 Picadilly & 6 New Coventry Street.

$2\frac{1}{2}''$ Cold Cream of Roses for the skin. BREIDENBACH & CO. perfumer, to her Majesty Prince Albert & Duchess of Kent, New Bond St.

$2\frac{3}{4}''$ Otto of Rose Cold Cream. S. F. Goss Ltd. 460 Oxford Street. W. & 201 Regent Street.

$2\frac{5}{8}$ Cold Cream of Roses. Lorimer & Co, trademark, arm holding globe, centre. Britannia Row, Islington.

$2\frac{3}{4}''$ J. B. Hay & Co. Cold Cream a la Rose, 6 New Coventry St.

$3''$ Cold Cream of Roses. CSSA, 136 Queen Victoria St., E.C.

$2\frac{3}{4}''$ Whitaker & Grossmith's Glycerine Cold Cream of Roses, 22 Silk Street, City of London.

$2\frac{3}{4}''$ Cold Cream of Roses. W. Ive, 115 Gloucester Road, Kensington.

$2\frac{3}{4}''$ Otto of Rose Cold Cream. S. F. Goss Ltd, London, W.

$2\frac{3}{4}''$ W. A. Goodall. Otto of Rose Cold Cream, Elm Park, Terrace, ornamental gold rim border.

$2\frac{1}{2}''$ Rose Cold Cream. Sussex Co-op, Drug Co. Ltd., 135 Queens Road, Brighton.

$2\frac{3}{4}''$ Otto of Rose Cold Cream. Wilson & Son, gold border.

$3''$ Cold Cream. Ornamental background scroll.

$2\frac{1}{4}''$ Cold Cream. Bradley & Bourdes, 6 Pont St., Belgrave Square, London.

$2\frac{1}{4}''$ Atkinson Rose Cold Cream. 1s., ornamental border (*no London.*)

$2\frac{3}{4}''$ Otto of Rose Cold Cream. S. Maw Son & Sons, London.

$3''$ R. S. Dampney. Cold Cream of Roses, Kensington.

$2\frac{3}{4}''$ B. Broome. Rose Cold Cream. Woodford Green & Caterham Hill.

$2\frac{7}{8}''$ Cold Cream of Roses. Young & Postens, 35 Baker St. London.

$2\frac{3}{4}''$ T. Chase. Cold Cream. Five Ways, Edgbastond, gold border.

$2\frac{3}{4}''$ Cold Cream. Boots Cash Chemists, Sheffield, Nottingham, London.

$2\frac{3}{4}''$ Sydney Rogers Cold Cream. Osbourne Road, Southsea, gold border.

$2\frac{1}{2}''$ Cold Cream perfumed with Otto of Roses. Coat of Arms.

Dunkley & Rogers. Cold Cream. Tunbridge Wells.

Hammerton. Cold Cream. Colchester.

Hardcastle. Otto of Rose. Brighton.

Robert L. Whigham. Rose Cold Cream.

Glaisyer. 53 Kings Road. Cold Cream.

Fielder & Co. Cold Cream. Newbury.

Actual size: 1 C; 2 D.

Actual size: 1 A; 2 C;
3 B; 4 B; 5 A; 6 C.

CARBOLIC
CARBOLIC ACID 3
TOOTH PASTE
FOR CLEANSING AND
S. MAW, SON & SONS. LONDON
TRADE MARK
PRESERVING THE TEETH & GUMS
S. MAW, SON & SONS
ALDERSGATE STREET
LONDON ENGLAND

1

S. MAW, SON & SONS
WHITE CHERRY
TOOTH PASTE
S. MAW, SON & SONS, LONDON
TRADE MARK
FOR CLEANING & PRESERVING
THE TEETH AND GUMS
ALDERSGATE STREET
LONDON
ENGLAND

2

MAW'S
INDIAN BETEL NUT OR ARECA
TOOTH PASTE
UNEQUALLED FOR ITS SALUTARY
EFFECTS ON THE
TRADE MARK
TEETH & GUMS
S. MAW, SON & SONS LTD
ALDERSGATE STREET
LONDON
& BARNET
ENGLAND

3

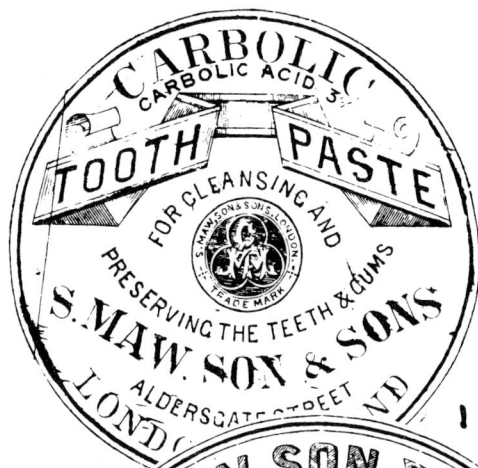

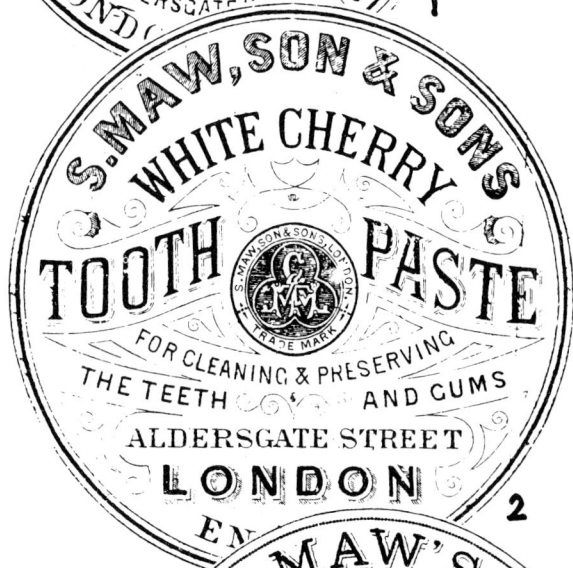

Actual size: 1 C; 2 D;
3 B.

70

GROUP C

Roberts & Co. Glycerine Cold Cream, gold band.
E. Worth. Bournemouth. Otto of Rose, gold band.
John Barker. Otto of Rose. 71 High St., Kensington.
Parkes Drug Stores. Otto of Rose Cold Cream, with trade mark.
Cold Cream of Roses. Parkes Drug Stores. Brixton.
B. Broome Cold Cream. Chelmsford & Woodford.
Hickman Sons & Metcalf. Otto of Rose Cold Cream. Newbury.
Richard & Constance. Otto of Rose Cold Cream.
Patey & Co. Cold Cream, late of 37 Lombard St.
John Bell & Co. Cold Cream. 255 Oxford Street.
Superior Cold Cream. Geo. Weston, 25 Parliament St., Harrogate.
Roberts & Co's. Cold Cream. 5 Rue de la Paix, Paris. GOLD BAND.
Roberts & Co's Cold Cream. 5 Rue de la Paix, Paris. GOLD BAND no ornamental
   border.
T. E. Handford. Otto of Rose Cold Cream. Harrogate.
Otto of Rose Cold Cream, square lid.
Cold Cream, ornamental background, large.
Beral–Paris. Cold Cream.
John Atkins. Otto of Rose Cold Cream. Bayswater.
Ball Pharmacist. Cold Cream. Southport. GOLD BAND
Saunders. Otto of Roses Cold Cream.
H. P. Withers. Rose Cold Cream. Blackpool.
Fisher & Co. Cold Cream. Leamington.
Townson & Co. Altringham & Bowden. Otto of Rose.
Parkes Drug Stores. Cold Cream of Roses. London.
William Crompton. Rose Cold Cream. Bury.
$3\frac{1}{2}''$ Ambrosial Shaving Cream. S. Maw Son & Thompson, London.
$3''$ Mrs. Ellen Hales Ointment. Brandon St. Walworth, London.
$3''$ Creme D'Amandes. R. Hovenden & Son Ltd, London.
$2\frac{3}{4}''$ Morris's Eye Ointment. Cure for All Diseases of the Eyes.
$2\frac{3}{8}''$ Josephson's Australian Ointment. Sydney. N.S.W.
$3\frac{1}{2}''$ Almond Shaving Cream, trademark centre, printed GREEN.
$3\frac{1}{2}''$ Vianes Shaving Cream. Maurice Viane. 30 Knightsbridge.
$3\frac{3}{4}''$ Ambrosial Shaving Cream. S. Maw & Sons.
$2''$ Eye Ointment, with open eye picture.
$3\frac{3}{8}''$ F. S. Cleaver. Saponaceous Shaving Cream Creme D'Amande.
Rooks Windsor Ointment. M. Rook (trade mark a Rook).
$3\frac{1}{2}''$ Creme D'Amande Shaving. Boots.

1

2

3

4

GROUP C

2½″ J. &. E. Atkinsons Glycerine Cream.
2″ Golden Eye Ointment and base.
2½″ Roger & Gallet Creme de Savon Pour La Barbe (Monogram lid with matching base) GREEN PRINT.
Glycerine & Honey Cream. Thomas Drug Stores, for chapped hands.
Wolff & Schwindt Karlsruha Schuppen Pomade.
The Dandriff Pomade. A. Hirst, Sheffield.
Creme de Savon aux Amandes Emeres. L.T. PIVER. PARIS.
T. F. Bristow & Co., Ltd. Shave Easy Shaving Soap. London. GREEN PRINT.
Douglas perfumer. 21 & 23 New Bond St., London, double border.
Douglas perfumer. 21 & 23 New Bond St., London, smaller with single border.

Holloways Ointment:
4s.6d. 3¾″ F; 3s.0d. E;
2s.9d. D.

Actual size: 1 C; 2 D;
3 B; 4 B.

ODONTINE

das Beste zur

Reinigung u. Erhaltung
der Zähne.

Louiser Drogerie

Emil Mitau

BERLIN.N.W.

LOUISEN STR.64.

1

DUNCAN FLOCKHART & Co

COLD
CREAM

EDINBURGH.

2

3

IMPERIAL CORALLINE

TOOTH PASTE

FREE FROM ACID OR ANY DELETERIOUS INGREDIENT.

SWEETENS THE BREATH.

CLEANS. PRESERVES. AND BEAUTIFIES THE

TEETH AND GUMS

PREPARED ONLY BY

ROBERTS & Co

Chemists

TO THE ENGLISH. RUSSIAN. AND AUSTRIAN AMBASSADORS.

23. PLACE VENDOME PARIS.

AND 76. NEW BOND ST. LONDON.

Actual size: 1 F; 2 C; 3 E.

GROUP D

$3\frac{3}{4}''$ FORNUM & MASON Caviar 182 & 183 Piccadilly, W. Royal Coat of Arms, no plumes. By Appointment to the King. (Edward VII).
$4''$ W. &. G. Buszard. Bride Cake Manufacturers, 197/199 Oxford St.
Civil Service Supply Assoc. Anchovy Paste.
Fortnum & Mason. Chicken & Ham.
Burgess Anchovy Paste. Solid Black Border variety.
Morel Bros. Cobbett & Son. Chicken & Ham. Inverness.
C. F. Sutton & Sons & Co. Kings Cross. Anchovy Paste.
Blanchflower Gorgona Anchovy Paste. Grt. Yarmouth.
$2\frac{1}{2}''$ Cherry Tooth Paste. Lorimer & Co., Britannia Row, Islington, arm holding globe and background cherries.
$3''$ Cherry. Durbin, ornamental background and border.
$2\frac{1}{2}''$ Cherry. McIsaac & Co. 165 Hagley Road, Birmingham.
$3''$ Breidenbachs Cherry Paste Extra Moist. 1578 New Bond St.
$2\frac{3}{4}''$ Cherry Tooth Paste. Parkes Drug Stores Ltd.
$2\frac{3}{4}''$ Saponaceous. Neve & Co. 12. Wellington Place, Hastings.
$3\frac{1}{8}''$ Carbolic Tooth Paste.
Lutons. British Toothpaste. Levenshulme.
Alba Rose Tooth Paste. Breidenbach & Co.
Carbolic Tooth Powder. C. W. Isaac Co., Clifton.
Saunders Red Cherry Tooth Paste. Liverpool.
Cherry Toothpaste. Prepared by Beidenbach for Francis & Son Ltd., Brixton.
Cherry Toothpaste. Prepared by Breidenbach for Copland & Lye. Glasgow.
T. Morson & Son. Cherry Tooth Paste. 124 Southampton Row.
Cherry Tooth Paste. S. Maw Son & Thompson, Aldersgate Street.
Cheery Tooth Paste. T. & S. London.
Areca Nut Tooth Paste. T. &. S. London.
Areca Nut Tooth Paste. C. S. S. A. Ltd., London.
Savars Areca Nut Toothpaste.
R. Thomas Areca Tooth Paste. 13 Upper Baker St.
F. S. Cleavers' Areca Nut Tooth Paste. 1/9 size.
T. F. Bristow & Co's. Areca Nut Tooth Paste.
Taylor & Cuthbert Carnation Toothpaste.
Areca Nut (Chauvin et Cie) tooth paste, pictorial cherries, & boat on lake.
Cherry Tooth Paste, ornamental design, large.
Army & Navy Stores. Cherry. London.
S. Maw & Son & Sons. White Cherry. London.
S. Maw Son & Thompson. Cherry. London.

1

2

3

4

5

6

7

8

HARROD'S

Telephone No
WESTERN ONE
60 Lines

HARRODS SERVE THE WORLD

Telegrams:
"EVERYTHING,
LONDON."

BLOATER PASTE

FOR

Toast. Biscuits.&c..

Harrods Ltd

87 to 135, BROMPTON ROAD. S.W.

1

FORTNUM & MASON LIMTD

DIEU ET MON DROIT

BY APPOINTMENT
TO THE KING

POTTED BEEF

182 & 183 Piccadilly. W.

2

YARMOUTH BLOATER PASTE

PREPARED WITH SELECTED FISH

TRADE MARK

THE YARMOUTH FISHING BOAT
BLANCHFLOWER

Manufacturer

SOLE PROPRIETOR OF THE CELEBRATED MANSION SAUCE

GREAT YARMOUTH

ENTERED AT STA HALL 1908

3

1 C; 2 D; 3 E.

1 B; 2 A; 3 B; 4, in blue,
E, 5 B; 6 E; 7 B; 8 D.

77

GROUP D

Benbow & Sons, Cherry. London.
D. Judson & Son. Areca Nut. London.
D. Judson & Son. Cherry Tooth Paste. London.
$2\frac{1}{2}''$ Otto of Rose Cold Cream, ornamental background bowl of flowers & floral border, registration mark dated 1876.
3" Sandringham Cold Cream. Daffodil design. PRINTED GREEN.
3" British Lanoline Cold Cream with trade mark.
Low Son & Haydon. London.
Cold Cream (Turquoise Green Print).
The Royal Cold Cream of Glycerine, prepared by Royal Perfumery, ornamental border. GREEN PRINT.
E. Rimmel Cold Cream of Roses. Oxendon St. Haymarket. BLUE PRINT.
3" Pomade pour Nettoyer les Cheveux, Curtis & Co., 48 Baker St.
$3\frac{1}{4}''$ Holloways Ointment. 2s. 9d.
$3\frac{1}{4}''$ Army & Navy Co-op. Soc. Ltd. Almond Shaving Cream. GREEN PRINT.
$1\frac{3}{4}''$ James Tidmarsh's Razer Paste. 6d.
3" Thorntons Celebrated Toilet Cream. A. P. Towle & Son.
$2\frac{3}{4}''$ Oatmeal Cream. John Solley. South Kensington.
Lancaster Universal Ointment.
Norris' Skin Pomade. Palmerston Road. Southsea.
Holloways Ointment. 533 Oxford St. 2s. 9d. size.
Mrs. Williams Pur Herbel Nutritive Cream. Leamington Spa.
Roger & Gallet Paris Creme D'Amandes Ameres Pour La Barbe.
Almond Perfumed Shaving Cream. Savars.
Rose Lipsalve. J. Atkins Bournemouth.
W. Cox. Medicated Glycerine & Quinine Pomade, London.
Doubledays Nutritive Toilet Cream. London.
Dr. Wrights Pearl Ointment. London. RED.
Old Doctor Hardys Celebrated Scorrutic Ointment. Wibsey.
Civil Service Co-operative Society. Rose Lip Salve London. RED.
3" Keys Restorative Dandriff Pomade. G. Key.

GROUP E

$3\frac{1}{2}''$ Anchovy Paste. Griffon style coat of arms.
$3\frac{3}{4}''$ Yarmouth Bloater Paste BLANCHFLOWER Gt. Yarmouth with fishing boat centre.
$3\frac{1}{2}''$ Anchovy Paste. Cross & Blackwell. 21 Soho Square, with coat of arms (Victoria).
$3\frac{3}{8}''$ Real Gorgona Anchovy Paste, coat of arms.
$3\frac{3}{4}''$ E. Lazenby & Son. Anchovy Paste. 6 Edward St., Portman Square.
Fortnum & Mason. Potted Game.
Fortnum & Mason. Potted Ham.
Burgess Anchovy Paste. (Larger size). Solid Black Border variety.
Carters Bloater Paste.
Blanchflower, Yarmouth. Bloater Paste.
Claytons Teraxacum or Dandelion Cocoa.
Hannells Real Gorgona Anchovy Paste, ornamental border.
$3''$ Dr. Ziemer's Alexandra with centre portrait of Alexandra.
$2\frac{5}{8}'' \times 3\frac{1}{2}''$ Dr. Delorme's Antiseptic & Preservative AMA ROSA (RED PRINTED Oval Lid).
$11\frac{1}{2}''$ Sample size Gosnell's Cherry Toothpaste. Extra Moist. John Gosnell & Co.
$1\frac{1}{2}''$ Sample size Gosnell's Cherry Toothpaste Extra Moist. John Gosnell & Company Limited.
$3\frac{1}{4}''$ Thornton Anthracoline 1/- pink background.
$3\frac{3}{4}'' \times 2\frac{1}{4}''$ Salicifrico Antiseptic Toothpaste W. Martindale, 10 New Cavendish St., London.
$3\frac{1}{4}''$ Cherry Crown Perfumery Co. Trademark crown centre.
$3\frac{1}{4}''$ Areca Nut Tooth Paste. Lorimer & Co., London & New York. Mosque Pictorial.
$3''$ Beddard's Belgravia Tooth Paste. T. C. White Esq., MRCS. Prepared by John Beddard, 46 Churton St., Belgrave Road, coat of arms top centre.
Cherry Tooth Paste. "BOVAL".
Cherry Tooth Paste. Crown Perfumery.
Woods Areca Nut 1/- Tooth Paste.
Okells Monatooth Paste.
Bell's Betal Nut Tooth Paste. Ferris & Co., Bristol, with coat or arms centre (GOLD BAND).
Wilcockson & Co. Hinckley. Cherry Tooth Paste.

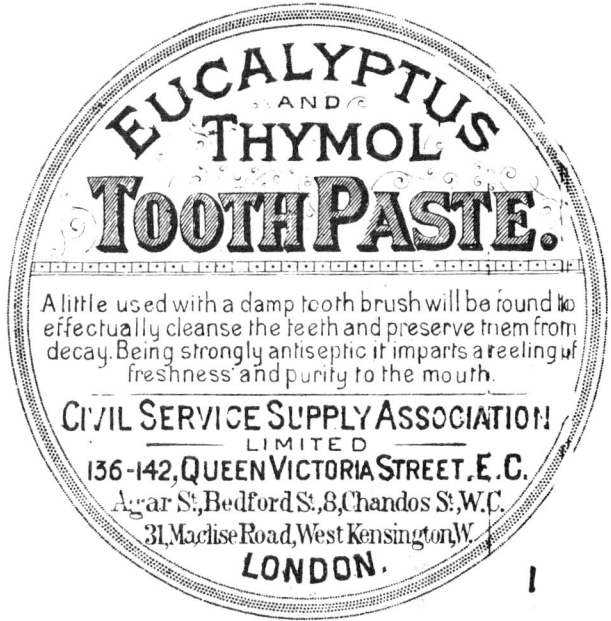

EUCALYPTUS AND THYMOL TOOTH PASTE.

A little used with a damp tooth brush will be found to effectually cleanse the teeth and preserve them from decay. Being strongly antiseptic it imparts a feeling of freshness and purity to the mouth.

CIVIL SERVICE SUPPLY ASSOCIATION
LIMITED
136-142, QUEEN VICTORIA STREET, E.C.
Agar St., Bedford St., 8, Chandos St., W.C.
31, Maclise Road, West Kensington, W.
LONDON.

1

1 4″ E; 2 4″ F.

Opposite, all group F:
1 "Eridge Castle";
2 "Christchurch, Hants";
3 "Canterbury Cathedral";
4 "Chichester Cathedral"; 5 "New Church of St. Nicholas, Guildford".

TREACHER & CO LIMITED
ANTISEPTIC
SUPARI OR BETEL NUT
TOOTH PASTE
TRADE MARK
PRESERVES THE TEETH
Gives tone and Colour to the Gums prevents Toothache and imparts a grateful fragrance to the Breath.
BOMBAY CHEMISTS POONA

2

GROUP E

Roberts & Co. Imperial Coralline Tooth Paste. GOLD BAND.
J. E. Robinson MPS. Elite Tooth Paste.
Benbow & Son. London. Areca Nut Toothpaste with pictorial design mosque & Areca Nut.
Cherry Tooth Paste. Loveitt & Co., Coventry. GOLD BAND
T. F. Bristow & Co. Cherry. London.
Saunders Areca Nut. Liverpool.
Ferris & Co. BELLS Betal Nut. Bristol. GOLD BAND.
Thompson, Walters Hole & Co., Ltd. Areca Nut. LONDON. Yellow.
Benbow & Sons. Cold Cream.
Ch. Jaschke's Cold Cream. Gold Band.
Icilma Cold Cream. floral design. BROWN PRINT.
Otto of Rose Cold Cream., with central floral design.
Rose Cold Cream. J. B. Barnes & Sons, 205 Knightsbridge. GOLD BAND.
$2\frac{1}{2}''$ James Atkinson Bears Grease, 24 Old Bond St., London. 2/6d.
$2''$ Fine Old Naples Soap. J. E. Atkinson. 2/6d.
Holloways Ointment. 3s 0d. size.
Special shaving cream. H. M. Lee, 9 Curzon St., Mayfair, London.
Reade Brothers & Co. Ltd. Egyptian Salve. Wolverhampton.
Army Navy Toilet Club. Pomade Sylphides. London. Gold Band.
Taylors Ointment. James D. Taylor, Huddersfield.

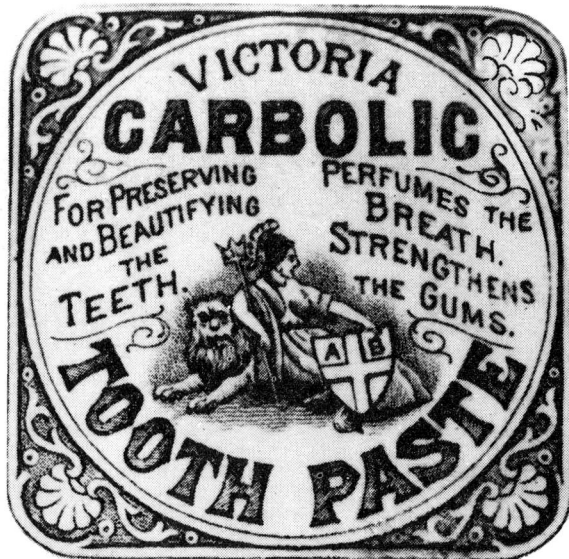

"Victoria Carbolic", E.

Actual size: 1 B; 2 B; 3 B; 4 B; 5 A.

1 gold on blue
background, G; 2 green
background, C; 3 G; 4
gold print, F; 5 $3\frac{7}{8}$" with
red background, G.

GROUP F

$2\frac{3}{4}''$ Toothpaste. Truly a magnificent pictorial lid showing trees & men in a boat shooting game.

Woods Areca Nut 1/-. MPS.

Thorntons Anthraoline. 1/6d size red background. LARGE.

F. C. Moss. Millar, Torquay. Areca Nut. 1/- size, marbled border.

The Chemist Assoc. Cherry Tooth Paste. Curtain Road, coloured lid (red, green, yellow) with cherry design.

Mona Tooth Paste Okells with Douglas Pier I. O. Man, centre.

Thymo Eucalyptus. GREEN.

Whitaker & Grossmith. Tooth Powder, London.

Jean Dupont. Cherry. London. BROWN.

Stone & Son. Cherry. Exeter. RED.

$2\frac{3}{8}''$ Sharp Brothers Cold Cream. 12 Southampton Row, London, with Harp trade mark and ornamental border. RED PRINTED LID.

Sharp Brothers Soap & Perfumery Co. Cold Cream. RED PRINT.

Chave & Jackson. Cucumber Winter Cream. Hereford. RED.

Blake Sandford & Black. Cold Cream. London. BLUE.

$3\frac{3}{4}''$ Mrs. Ellen Hales Celebrated Heal All Ointment. Brandon St., Walworth, London.

Icilma Creme de Savon Pour La Barbe. BROWN PRINT.

Holloways Ointment. 533 Oxford St. 4s. 6d. size.

Circassian Cream. Skelton, Late Honey & Skelton, black background with Prince of Wales Feathers design.

F. S. Cleaver's Genuine Bears Grease. 6d.

Russian Bears Grease. Price & Co.

Small pictorial lid of Queens Head in Gold on white background.

Small pictorial lid of Queens Head in Gold on blue background.

"Genuine Yarmouth
Bloater Paste", F.

GROUP G

$3\frac{7}{8}''$ Dr. Posteels Cherry Tooth Paste for Beautifying and Preserving the Teeth and Gums, centre trademark Queen Victoria Jubilee style head two crowns, left and right. Cerise colour background.

Cordelier, Sittingbourne. Areca Nut Cherry Tooth Paste (view of Sittingbourne Church with ornamental border).

Cordelier, Sittingbourne. Areca Nut Cherry Tooth Paste (view of Sittingbourne Church. No Border).

Yardleys Tooth Paste. Coloured cherries.

Gosnell Bros. & Co. Universal Cherry Tooth Paste. GREEN BACKGROUND.

Sandringham Cherry Tooth Paste. Pictorial Lid.

C. Pierrepont. Superfine American Dentifrice. Bolton, oblong lid with eagle design.

Dr. Ziemer's Alexandra Tooth Paste pictorial with gold border.

Price & Gosnell Cold Cream (Napoleon Price).

$3''$ Genuine Russian Bears Grease For Increasing Growth of the Hair (2 bears with wide ornamental border) CONNOISSEUR LID.

Swifts Hair Regenerator. C. H. Swift, Huddersfield.

Patey & Co. Genuine Bears Grease. 37 Lombard St.

Atkinson's Bears Grease. 24 Old Bond St. Price 5s.

Henry Burton. Perfumer. 18 Greek St.

Simpsons Pomade Depurative. W. Simpson, Stockton, marbled lid.

John Gosnell & Co. Ambrosial Shaving Co., marbled lid.

Williams Swiss Violet Shaving Cream. J. D. Williams Co. Glastonbury. Conn Genuine Yankee Shaving Soap. LILAC GREEN & BROWN PRINT.

James Atkinsons Bears Grease, Bear in chains. 4s size.

Patey & Co. Genuine Bears Grease, ornamental border. Bear with rope.

Genuine Bears Grease, bear sitting down in centre of lid with ornamental border Miniature Lid. EARLY & RARE.

Genuine Russian Bears Grease, Pictorial Bear with Cub.

Ambrosial Shaving Cream. John Gosnell & Co., patronized by Prince Albert.

Rimmel's Saponaceous Cream of Almonds, 96, Strand & Cornhill, Dark fawn with white deckled edge.

Genuine Russian Bears Grease, pictorial two bears.

Swift's Hair Regenerator. Huddersfield.

Genuine Russian Bears Grease. London.

COLLECTING

POT LID LADIES

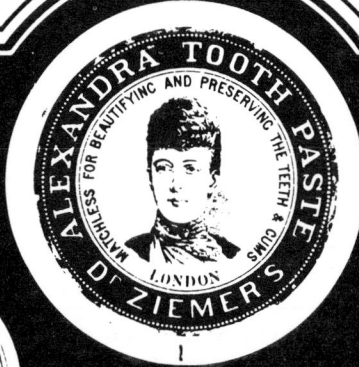

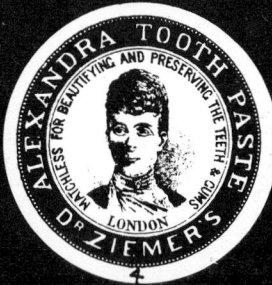

1 C; 2 C, red or green print D; 3 C; 4 C; 5 red print, F; 6 C; 7 Yellow background, red cherries, F; 8 B.

Opposite, from the collection of David Lewis: 1 F; 2 F; 3 XXX; 4 F; 5 F; 6 F; 7 F; 8 G; 9 G.

GROUP XXX   .

$2\frac{1}{4}''$ Price & Gosnells Bears Grease for the growth of hair from the animal in its
  Native Climate. BLUE PRINTED LID with bear.
Rimmel's Bears Grease. London & Paris. BLUE PRINT.

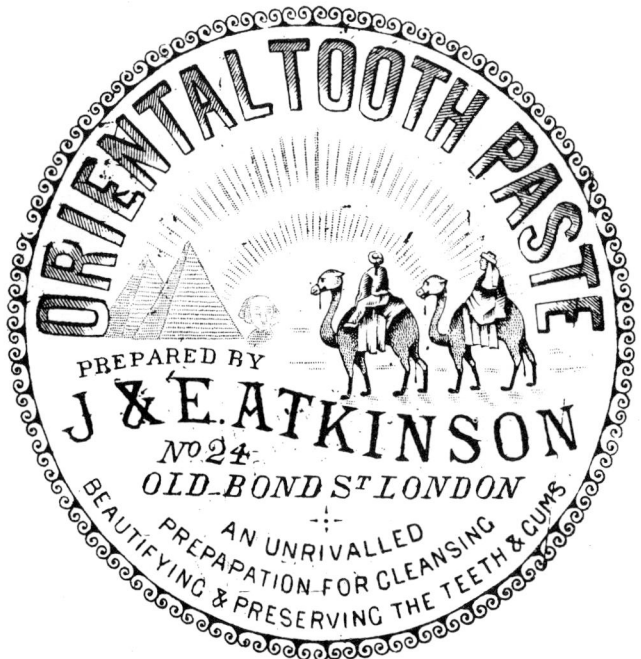

"J. E. Atkinson" $3\frac{1}{8}'' - E.$

*Opposite: 1 E; 2 G; 3 blue
print, G; 4 G; 5 blue print,
G; 6 G; 7 G; 8 F.*

Enlargement, showing details of original engraving, 2s 6d. D; 5s 0d. F; 10s. 0d. and £1 0s. 0d. F.

"Englands Pride", black background, 3 star; green background, 5 star.

Useful Information

The Pot-Lid Circle
Secretary: A. Ball
15 Arden Road
Nuneaton
Warwickshire

The Society aims to stimulate interest and encourage research into underglaze prints on Staffordshire pot-lids, plates, jars, etc. Regular meetings are held and newsletters and a journal are published from time to time.

British Antique Bottle Collectors Club
72 Humber Avenue
Coventry
West Midlands

Established in 1976. The aim of the club is to promote bottle and pot-lid collecting and bring together collectors from all parts of the world. Insurance, information, and directory services available.

Antique Bottle Collecting
Chapel House Farm
Newport Road
Albrighton
Nr. Wolverhampton

Britain's only glossy covered monthly magazine on the hobbies of collecting pot-lids, bottles, clay pipes, dolls heads, coins, medals, artefacts, and other Victorian relics. Read all over the world and has many regular features, photographs and articles by prominent authors.

Displays of pot-lids open to the public are to be found at:
Ashmolean Museum, Oxford.
Fitzwilliam Museum, Cambridge.
Laing Art Gallery and Museum, Newcastle-Upon-Tyne.
Museum and Art Gallery, Swindon.

Other books from MAB Publishing

Information, articles, trends, clubs, books, exhibitions, etc. for 60 collecting hobbies. 200 pages, illustrated throughout. Forward by Richard Lay – Antiques Correspondent of the *Daily Mail*. A book no collector can afford to be without. £2.50.

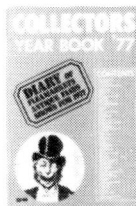

A companion volume to "Antique Glass Bottles" covering a wider selection of bottles plus general sections on finding, identifying and investing in bottles. Over 1,500 bottles priced. Provides information for collectors, investors, dealers, auctioneers, and museums on one of Britains fastest growing hobbies. £1.95.

Over 200 photographs and illustrations of different bottles and prices of hundreds more. Easy to read. Formula for valuing many types of bottles. Baby feeders, beers, codds, fire extinguishers, gins, ginger beers, hamiltons, inks, internal stoppers, medicines, mineral waters, perfumes, poisons, sealed bottles all included. £1.85.

The first book devoted solely to sealed bottles since "Ruggles-Brise" (1949). Provides answers to many questions surrounding the age, origin and ownership of sealed bottles and traces development of English wine bottles. 120 pages including over 100 photographs and illustrations of seals and sealed bottles, many of which have never been published before. £4.50.

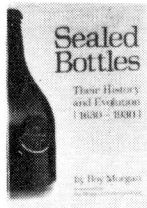

Available from your bookseller or from the publishers

**MAB PUBLISHING,
458c, STANTON ROAD,
BURTON-ON-TRENT, STAFFS**

Acknowledgements

I wish to thank the following for their assistance in supplying information and material for this book:

Peter Bettis of "Joan Allen's Collector's Old Bottle Room" for providing prices and information concerning black and white pot lids.

Roger Green, editor and publisher of *Antique Bottle Collecting*.

Gordon Litherland for photographs.